Rupert Brooke's
GRANTCHESTER

Text by Francis Burkitt and Christine Jennings, and photographs by Christine Jennings.

Francis Burkitt's family moved from Cambridge to Grantchester in 1928, and he and his children are now the third and fourth generations to live in the village.

Christine and her late husband Robbie Jennings arrived in Grantchester in 1961, and their children grew up in the village.

This book is dedicated to Francis' wife Jo and their three children; and to Christine's three children and nine grandchildren.

All proceeds will be passed to good causes in the village.

ISBN 978-0-9544818-3-4

Grantchester, about two miles up-stream from Cambridge, is perhaps one of the most famous villages in England, loved by many for its rural setting and beautiful meadows along the riverbank.

The young poet and idealist Rupert Brooke was one of those who fell under Grantchester's spell. While visiting Germany in 1912 aged 25, "sweating, sick and hot", he ached for what he remembered as a golden summer the year before, when he had lodged in rooms in the village whilst studying at King's College.

1911 had been one of those legendary long, hot English summers, so hot that Rupert had been able to persuade the future novelist Virginia Woolf to bathe naked with him in the River Granta.

At the time of writing the poem, Rupert was deeply troubled, in turmoil over his political sympathies, his sexuality and his creativity. This all bursts forth in his poem as anguish, self-mockery and the technical business of poetic self-expression – and results in what he called "a masterpiece", and in what we delight in as a paean of praise for the English countryside and way of life in general, and for the village of Grantchester in particular.

The poem begins "Just now the lilac is in bloom..."

Two walkers climb up the river bank into the village; near this spot was the first crossing of the river, in Roman and Saxon times

A brief history of Grantchester

Dinosaurs once roamed the meadows and fields round Grantchester – we know that because their dung, called coprolite, was found in fields around the village and mined from 1870–1890 and later during the First Word War, with the phosphate that it contained being used for fertilisers and munitions.

The historian Coneybeare, a contemporary of Rupert Brooke's, mentioned in his *Highways & Byways of Cambridgeshire* that bones of the mammoth and woolly rhinocerous had been found in the fields around the village, indicating that many millennia ago the region passed through a period of arctic temperatures; and that a few miles up-river hippopotamus and African rhinocerous bones had been found, so the region must also have gone through sub-tropical periods.

Grantchester was the site of Roman and then Anglo-Saxon settlements, and there was a ford through the river, which at this point is called the Granta. It was first called Cair-granta (the castle on the Granta), and later Granta-sete (the town on the Granta). The river-crossing at Grantchester pre-dates the bridge downstream, where the river changes its name to the Cam, by many centuries.

Around 700 AD the Venerable Bede called the village "a desolate little city". It is also mentioned in the Doomsday Book (1086) and fragments of the church are Norman.

Three colleges have dominated the village's history – Merton College, Oxford; Corpus Christi College, Cambridge; and King's College, Cambridge.

Walter de Merton (1205 – 1277) bought land when he educated students in The School of Pythagoras in Cambridge, about a decade before the University itself was founded. When he founded Merton College, Oxford in 1264, his endowments to the college included his land in Grantchester; the College has since sold almost all of this, although it still retains one last property in the village.

Shortly after its foundation in 1352, Corpus Christi College became Patron of the living, giving it the right to appoint the vicars, which it retains to this day.

In 1452 King's College became Lord of the Manor and gradually acquired most of the farmland around the village, including the world-famous Meadows, which it still owns.

The Victorian resident Samuel Page Widnall, writing in his *A History of Grantchester in the County of Cambridge*, notes that Queen Elizabeth I processed through the village on 5 August 1564, on her way to a visit to Cambridge.

The Grantchester that Rupert Brooke knew was a quiet place, with most of the community working on the land or in the large flour mill over the river. Traffic was largely horse-drawn, water was pumped from wells, and lighting came from candles or oil-lamps.

In the 1960s a housing estate was built by the Council, considerably enlarging the population. Today the village has approximately 250 houses and 650 residents, but still retains the rural character that countless previous generations knew and loved.

Grantchester is blessed with four pubs:
the Rupert Brooke (formerly the Rose & Crown), the Green Man, the Red Lion and the Blue Ball.

Village houses:
Manor House (owned by King's College), Grant Cottages, the former Alms Houses and The White Cottage

King's College, Cambridge, where Brooke was an undergraduate and later a Fellow

Rupert Brooke (1887 – 1915)

Rupert Brooke stood out among his contemporaries – for his looks, his vivacity, his questing intellect searching for ultimate values, his uncertainty in love, and his self-mockery . . . in short, he had the temperament of a true poet. Furious at his frequent breakdowns in health, yet physically courageous; volatile in relationships, yet dependent on loyal friends . . . he himself was aware of the painful process of growing up, and it was only when he experienced the horrors of the Great War that he felt at last settled and purposeful.

Brooke was born in Rugby in Warwickshire, where his father was a housemaster at the famous public school. He was educated at the local preparatory school and, just after his fourteenth birthday, entered his father's house at Rugby School. He was clever and good at rugby and cricket, but was principally noted for his emerging literary talent – he wrote poetry, founded a literary magazine, debated, and won prizes for his writing.

From Rugby, Brooke won a classics scholarship to King's College, Cambridge, where his father had been a Fellow and his uncle was Dean and later Provost. The tripos centred on the study of ancient Greece and Rome, and he found the transition from Rugby to Cambridge difficult and never did particularly well in his university exams. However, it also included lectures on literature, philosophy and art, which appealed to him. In his first year, he had a minor part in a Greek play; in his second he produced and took a leading part in Milton's *Comus*; and later he acted in *Faustus* by Marlowe, the 16th Century Elizabethan dramatist and contemporary of Shakespeare, which led to the founding of the University Marlowe Dramatic Society, which still flourishes today.

Brooke's acting roles helped bring him in contact with a growing circle of friends: undergraduates, those senior to him, and others based in London. Through them, he encountered two societies that quickly shaped his views on life.

First, he was elected to the select University society known as The Apostles, an intellectual discussion group which advocated a break from the formality of Victorian conventions and promoted tolerance, open-mindedness, critical thinking and self-examination. Second, he became a member and later President of the University branch of the Fabian Society. The Fabians had been founded in London in 1844 to champion social reform, to free land and commerce from individual and class ownership, and to promote the "rights of man" and equality of men and women.

Brooke's striking good looks and golden hair often attracted comment. He was considered to be a "young Apollo" (after the Greek god of the sun); the poet W. B. Yeats said he was "the handsomest young man in England"; and James Strachey (brother of the writer Lytton) said "he's so beautiful he's hardly human". His wide and varied circle of friends included the writers E. M. Forster, Henry James and Virginia Woolf; the poet W. B. Yeats; the playwright George Bernard Shaw; the economist John Maynard Keynes; the artists Augustus John and Gwen Raverat; and Violet Asquith, daughter of the Prime Minister.

Brooke's lack of focus on his academic work meant that he only achieved a second-class degree, and his Tutor suggested he should move out of town for his fourth year, to enable him to concentrate more on his studies and face less distraction from his friends.

Accordingly in 1909 he took rooms in Grantchester in a former farmhouse called The Orchard, moving next door to The Old Vicarage a year later. There he worked on his thesis to support his attempt to be elected to a prize Fellowship at King's, and wrote a number of poems, many about emotional relationships and platonic concepts, all the while trying to find his own true poetical "voice". But he kept up his many friendships, had a continual stream of visitors, and hosted a succession of meals, discussion groups and readings. This was a serenely happy time of his life, and he wrote that Grantchester was "the place where I am happier than anywhere".

Through the Fabians, Brooke had met Katherine ("Ka") Cox, who was the Society's Treasurer, and his relationship with her came to affect much of the rest of his life. Each of them fell in and out of love with the other a number of times but, tragically for both of them, they were rarely in love with each other at the same time. In January 1912, just after Ka had rejected him for someone else, Brooke suffered a severe emotional and nervous breakdown. His doctor recommended rest and sunshine, and he went to the south of France and later Germany. During a short break back in England he learned that he had not been successful in obtaining his longed-for Fellowship. He returned to Germany in April, and waited for Ka, with whom he had been reconciled, to join him. It was there he wrote *The Old Vicarage, Grantchester*, which he perhaps started as a verse letter to her.

In March 1913 he was elected a Fellow at his second attempt, and shortly after embarked on a year-long-trip, touring the USA and Canada, funded by writing for a newspaper.

His travels also took him across the Pacific as far as Fiji and New Zealand; he lingered for three months in Tahiti before his return journey. While away he was often troubled by infections in small wounds – the septicaemia (blood poisoning) from which he was later to die.

After the start of the First World War, Brooke, aged 27, joined the Royal Naval Volunteer Reserve and in October 1914 was posted to join the (unsuccessful) defence of Antwerp in Belgium. He was severely affected by the sight of the half million refugees who fled the city as it was evacuated ahead of the advancing enemy army, describing it as "like Hell, a Dantesque Hell, terrible". This changed his attitude to the war; having joined up largely out of a sense of duty, he now saw the war as a great and vital exercise in moral purpose.

Back in Britain, he wrote and published a number of war poems, including *The Soldier*, with its haunting first lines, "If I should die, think only this of me: that there's some corner of a foreign field that is forever England".

In 1915 he set sail with his fellow troops to the Dardanelles in Turkey with the ultimate aim of capturing Constantinople (now Istanbul), but was re-routed to Egypt, where he suffered from sunstroke and dysentery. He was offered a staff (i.e. non-combatant) appointment, but characteristically refused it. His troop-ship then sailed to the island of Skyros off Greece, where he developed septicaemia from an insect bite, and died on St George's Day, 23 April. He was buried in an olive grove on the island.

Brooke was the first Fellow of a Cambridge College to die on active service in the war. His obituary in *The Times* was written by Winston Churchill.

Red Poll rare-breed cattle on Grantchester Meadows

The Old Vicarage, Grantchester

Cafe des Westens, Berlin, May 1912

Just now the lilac is in bloom,
All before my little room;
And in my flower-beds, I think,
Smile the carnation and the pink;
And down the borders, well I know,
The poppy and the pansy blow . . .

Oh! there the chestnuts, summer through,
Beside the river make for you
A tunnel of green gloom, and sleep
Deeply above; and green and deep
The stream mysterious glides beneath,
Green as a dream and deep as death.

— Oh, damn! I know it! and I know
How the May fields all golden show,
And when the day is young and sweet,
Gild gloriously the bare feet
That run to bathe . . .

    . . . *Du lieber Gott!*
Here am I, sweating, sick, and hot,
And there the shadowed waters fresh
Lean up to embrace the naked flesh.

Temperamentvoll German Jews
Drink beer around; — and *there* the dews
Are soft beneath a morn of gold.
Here tulips bloom as they are told;
Unkempt about those hedges blows
An English unofficial rose;

And there the unregulated sun
Slopes down to rest when day is done,
And wakes a vague unpunctual star,
A slippered Hesper; and there are
Meads towards Haslingfield and Coton
Where *das Betreten*'s not *verboten*.

ειθε γενοιμην . . . would I were
In Grantchester, in Grantchester! —

Some, it may be, can get in touch
With Nature there, or Earth, or such.
And clever modern men have seen
A Faun a-peeping through the green,
And felt the Classics were not dead,
To glimpse a Naiad's reedy head,
Or hear the Goat-foot piping low: . . .

But these are things I do not know.
I only know that you may lie
Day long and watch the Cambridge sky,
And, flower-lulled in sleepy grass,
Hear the cool lapse of hours pass,
Until the centuries blend and blur
In Grantchester, in Grantchester . . .

Still in the dawnlit waters cool
His ghostly Lordship swims his pool,
And tries the strokes, essays the tricks,
Long learnt on Hellespont, or Styx.

Dan Chaucer hears his river still
Chatter beneath a phantom mill.
Tennyson notes, with studious eye,
How Cambridge waters hurry by . . .

And in that garden, black and white,
Creep whispers through the grass all night;
And spectral dance, before the dawn,
A hundred Vicars down the lawn;
Curates, long dust, will come and go
On lissom, clerical, printless toe;
And oft between the boughs is seen
The sly shade of a Rural Dean . . .

Till, at a shiver in the skies,
Vanishing with Satanic cries,
The prim ecclesiastic rout
Leaves but a startled sleeper-out,
Grey heavens, the first bird's drowsy calls,
The falling house that never falls.

God! I will pack, and take a train,
And get me to England once again!
For England's the one land, I know,
Where men with Splendid Hearts may go;
And Cambridgeshire, of all England,
The shire for Men who Understand;
And of THAT district I prefer
The lovely hamlet Grantchester.

For Cambridge people rarely smile,
Being urban, squat, and packed with guile;
And Royston men in the far South
Are black and fierce and strange of mouth;
At Over they fling oaths at one,
And worse than oaths at Trumpington,
And Ditton girls are mean and dirty,
And there's none in Harston under thirty,

And folks in Shelford and those parts
Have twisted lips and twisted hearts,
And Barton men make Cockney rhymes,
And Coton's full of nameless crimes,
And things are done you'd not believe
At Madingley on Christmas Eve.

Strong men have run for miles and miles,
When one from Cherry Hinton smiles;
Strong men have blanched, and shot their wives,
Rather than send them to St. Ives;
Strong men have cried like babes, bydam,
To hear what happened at Babraham.

But Grantchester! ah, Grantchester!
There's peace and holy quiet there,
Great clouds along pacific skies,
And men and women with straight eyes,
Lithe children lovelier than a dream,
A bosky wood, a slumbrous stream,
And little kindly winds that creep
Round twilight corners, half asleep.

In Grantchester their skins are white;
They bathe by day, they bathe by night
The women there do all they ought;
The men observe the Rules of Thought.
They love the Good; they worship Truth;
They laugh uproariously in youth;
(And when they get to feeling old,
They up and shoot themselves, I'm told) . . .

Ah God! to see the branches stir
Across the moon at Grantchester!
To smell the thrilling-sweet and rotten
Unforgettable, unforgotten
River-smell, and hear the breeze
Sobbing in the little trees.

Say, do the elm-clumps greatly stand
Still guardians of that holy land?
The chestnuts shade, in reverend dream,
The yet unacademic stream?

Is dawn a secret shy and cold
Anadyomene, silver-gold?
And sunset still a golden sea
From Haslingfield to Madingley?
And after, ere the night is born,
Do hares come out about the corn?

Oh, is the water sweet and cool,
Gentle and brown, above the pool?
And laughs the immortal river still
Under the mill, under the mill?

Say, is there Beauty yet to find?
And Certainty? and Quiet kind?
Deep meadows yet, for to forget
The lies, and truths, and pain? . . . oh! yet

Stands the Church clock at ten to three?
And is there honey still for tea?

A clump of wild poppies

A view of the corn-fields in late summer

The Old Vicarage, Grantchester

Cafe des Westens, Berlin, May 1912

Brooke wrote this poem in Berlin, sitting in the Cafe des Westens. All his life he wrote a never-ending stream of letters to his friends, often interspersed with poetry, and it has been suggested that the poem perhaps started as a verse letter to Ka Cox. He had earlier written to her "I've a fancy you may be, just now, in Grantchester. I envy you, frightfully. That river and the chestnuts come back to me a lot". The poem was published in June in the King's College undergraduate magazine Basileon *(named after a Greek word for "king") to whose editor Rupert had immodestly telegraphed "a masterpiece is on its way".*

What are we to make of the poem? When it was first published, it was entitled The Sentimental Exile, *which gives a better clue to Brooke's feelings than the title a friend persuaded him to adopt a few months later. It is notable that he names no people and no buildings in the poem, and he can't have been longing for the company of the villagers of Grantchester since he had not mixed with them. Instead, in a life of ill-health, intellectual self-searching, emotional upheaval, continual oversight (Father, Uncle, Mother), academic stress, frequent exhaustion and emotional upheaval, the months he had spent living in Grantchester had been a time of relative peace, surrounded by good friends, working and entertaining contentedly, and espousing his political beliefs. Grantchester therefore represented, in his own words, "the place where I am happier than anywhere", and it is no wonder that he was sentimental about it as he thought of England and waited for Ka to join him from there.*

The poem is both serious and comic. When a schoolboy, he had written "When I say what I mean, people tell me 'O Rupert, what delightful nonsense you talk!' and when I venture on the humorous, I am taken seriously and very promptly and thoroughly squashed for 'saying such strange things'". But Brooke had become a master of combining the two, and in this poem the humour cloaks the seriousness of his longing, and the earnestness of his descriptions and questions is made light by the comic references. It is both light- and heavy-hearted, expressing a yearning for past happiness and the village that supplied it.

Brooke lodged in two houses in Grantchester; first at The Orchard and later next door at The Old Vicarage, which is shown here

Just now the lilac is in bloom,

All before my little room;

And in my flower-beds, I think,

Smile the carnation and the pink;

And down the borders, well I know,

The poppy and the pansy blow . . .

On this and the next two pages, Brooke, sitting in Berlin in May, imagines what the garden and countryside would then be like back home.

His "little room" refers to one of the three rooms he rented in The Old Vicarage, two downstairs and one upstairs.

On this page, his imagination starts close-by and moves progressively further away: he starts with the lilac blossom outside his room's window; then thinks about the nearby flower-beds; and lastly he recalls the flower borders, further down the garden.

Lilac, carnations, poppies and pansies

Oh! there the chestnuts, summer through,

Beside the river make for you

A tunnel of green gloom, and sleep

Deeply above; and green and deep

The stream mysterious glides beneath,

Green as a dream and deep as death.

Brooke remembers the line of chestnut trees at the bottom of his garden, which created an avenue or "tunnel of green gloom" beside the river, their branches overhanging the "green and deep" and "mysterious" river.

The line of chestnut trees still stands along the riverbank, and continues to shade the river

— Oh, damn! I know it! and I know

How the May fields all golden show,

And when the day is young and sweet,

Gild gloriously the bare feet

That run to bathe . . .

Brooke's imagination now runs further afield, and he thinks of the wider countryside – the fields glowing golden, perhaps reflecting the bright yellow colour of wild buttercups.

He also remembers how he had often, at dawn, run over the fields to swim in the river, his bare feet gilded with the golden pollen of the buttercups.

24

Golden buttercups and white cow parsley flower alongside a path across the meadows, leading down to the river

. . . Du lieber Gott!

Here am I, sweating, sick, and hot,

And there the shadowed waters fresh

Lean up to embrace the naked flesh.

Brooke complains of being in Germany – he swears in German, "Du lieber Gott" meaning "dear God" or "good heavens".

In the first of three pairs of contrasts, he compares Berlin ("here") with Grantchester ("there"). On this page, he contrasts the sweating heat of urban Berlin with the coolness of the river "embracing the . . . flesh" of a naked swimmer.

A scene of "shadowed waters" on the river in Grantchester

Temperamentvoll German Jews

Drink beer around; — and there the dews

Are soft beneath a morn of gold.

Here tulips bloom as they are told;

Unkempt about those hedges blows

An English unofficial rose;

Next, he compares his surroundings: in Berlin, he is surrounded by "temperamenvoll" (temperamental or surly) drinkers; in Grantchester, he would find soft morning dew. There is a further contrast between the two liquids: beer and dew drops.

Lastly, he contrasts formal straight-standing Continental tulips with informal English roses.

An unkempt English dog-rose flowers in a hedgerow

And there the unregulated sun

Slopes down to rest when day is done,

And wakes a vague unpunctual star,

A slippered Hesper; and there are

Meads towards Haslingfield and Coton

Where *das Betreten*'s not *verboten*.

And finally in this section of the poem, Brooke completes the day, moving to evening and nightfall, preferring the "unregulated" and "unpunctual" English timekeeping to the regimented formality of Germany.

Hesper is another name for Venus, the evening star. Meads are grass meadows. Haslingfield and Coton are neighbouring villages.

Brooke closes with one more contrast: "Das Betreten verboten" is German for "keep off the grass" or "no trespassing" which, he comments, does not apply to the rural English meads.

Dusk over the Grantchester fields

ειθε γενσιμην . . . would I were

In Grantchester, in Grantchester! —

Brooke now heaves a huge sigh from the bottom of his heart, and breaks into ancient Greek and exclaims ειθε γενσιμην, pronounced "eithe genoimen" and meaning "would I were". His homesickness is such that he's not happy merely imagining the scene back home – he wants to be there.

His use of this Greek phrase echoes an epigram of Plato's, expressing his love for his recently-deceased pupil Aster, which Brooke, given his classical eduction, would surely have known:

Asteras eisathreis, Aster emos.	*You gaze at stars, my Star.*
Eithe genoimen ouranos,	*Would that I were born the starry sky,*
'os pollois ommasin eis se blepo.	*that I with many eyes might gaze at you.*

Wright's Row, a row of ancient cottages in the centre of the village

Some, it may be, can get in touch

With Nature there, or Earth, or such.

And clever modern men have seen

A Faun a-peeping through the green,

And felt the Classics were not dead,

To glimpse a Naiad's reedy head,

Or hear the Goat-foot piping low: . . .

Brooke laughs at himself – he would have considered himself a "clever modern man" and, as a classicist, he might well have imagined fauns, naiads and Pan in Grantchester.

Fauns were spirits of wild woodland in Roman mythology; they had human bodies above the waist and goat-like bodies below. Naiads were a type of nymph (female spirits) in Greek mythology; they lived in streams and rivers, so might have reeds in their hair. The "Goat-foot" is the Greek God Pan, half-man and half-goat, and god of fields, woods and rustic music; he played "pan pipes", a primitive mouth organ made of hollow reeds.

But overleaf, he's going to say that these are not in fact his own reasons for loving the village.

A stream near Byron's Pool, where fauns and naiads might lurk behind the reeds and trees

But these are things I do not know.

I only know that you may lie

Day long and watch the Cambridge sky,

And, flower-lulled in sleepy grass,

Hear the cool lapse of hours pass,

Until the centuries blend and blur

In Grantchester, in Grantchester . . .

Brooke's passion for Grantchester has nothing to do with ancient mythology – what he likes is the rural scenery and countryside.

A dramatic May-time "Cambridge sky" towers above a hedgerow

Still in the dawnlit waters cool

His ghostly Lordship swims his pool,

And tries the strokes, essays the tricks,

Long learnt on Hellespont, or Styx.

Brooke now remembers events many centuries ago, and mentions three famous English poets and their connections with Grantchester.

"His ghostly Lordship" is long-dead Lord Byron (1788 – 1824) who, whilst an undergraduate at Cambridge, swam in the river above Grantchester at a spot now called Byron's Pool. From 1809 – 1811 he went on a Grand Tour of Europe. On 3 May 1810, aged 22 and in Constantinople (now called Istanbul), he swam the 4-mile stretch of sea called the Hellespont (now called the Dardanelles), which separates Europe and Asia. Byron is venerated as a national hero in Greece. By supreme irony, both Byron and Brooke died of fevers contracted whilst preparing to sail from Greece to fight against the Ottoman Empire.

The River Styx, in Greek mythology, was the river which formed the boundary between earth and the underworld.

Byron's Pool, on the river about a mile south of Grantchester.
Rupert frequently swam here, often at night, most famously in 1911 with Virginia Woolf, both "quite naked".

Dan Chaucer hears his river still

Chatter beneath a phantom mill.

Tennyson notes, with studious eye,

How Cambridge waters hurry by . . .

Two more poets now.

First Geoffrey Chaucer (1348 – 1400); "Dan" was a respectful way of addressing a person in his days, from the Latin word "dominus", meaning lord or master. The Reeve's Tale *is the third of Chaucer's* Canterbury Tales. *A reeve was a local official, and the tale starts:*

> At Trumpington, not far from Cambridge,
> There goes a brook, and over that a bridge,
> Upon the which brook there stands a mill;
> And this is absolute truth that I tell you.

That mill was probably near Byron's Pool, between Grantchester and Trumpington.

The reference to Lord Tennyson (1809 – 1890) may be to a poem he wrote called The Miller's Daughter. *Tennyson had been an undergraduate at Trinity College, Cambridge in the 1820s and was one of the earliest members of the Apostles, a society to which Brooke was later elected.*

The Old Mill straddles the river, with the mill pond before it

And in that garden, black and white,

Creep whispers through the grass all night;

And spectral dance, before the dawn,

A hundred Vicars down the lawn;

Curates, long dust, will come and go

On lissom, clerical, printless toe;

And oft between the boughs is seen

The sly shade of a Rural Dean . . .

Brooke now turns back to his lodging-house, The Old Vicarage, and recalls all its earlier religious inhabitants. The Old Vicarage dates from the 17th century, though it is possible that a former rectory had stood there before c. 1400. He dreams of them as ghosts in the garden in the middle of the night – in fact, the Ward family, later residents of the house, claimed to have seen ghosts and felt the presence of a poltergeist, so perhaps there is more to Brooke's dream than first appears.

Curates are assistants to the vicar; the Rural Dean is a senior vicar who presides over the Deanery, a group of neighbouring parishes.

The garden of The Old Vicarage in moonlight, with some spectral figures dancing

Till, at a shiver in the skies,

Vanishing with Satanic cries,

The prim ecclesiastic rout

Leaves but a startled sleeper-out,

Grey heavens, the first bird's drowsy calls,

The falling house that never falls.

As the dawn breaks and the "skies shiver", the vicars disappear with curses, leaving behind "a startled sleeper-out" – presumably Brooke himself, camping in a tent in the garden – under the grey morning sky, listening to the birds sing the dawn chorus.

Village tradition has it that the "falling house" refers to Garner Cottage, near where Brooke lived, whose over-hanging gable end always seems to be about to fall down, but never quite does. But it is more likely to refer to the folly at the bottom of The Old Vicarage's garden, which Brooke described in a letter as "a sham ruin; built fifty years ago" by the previous owner, Samuel Widnall, who "used to feast there nightly, with . . . I don't know whom. But they still do, spectrally, in the evenings; with faint lights and odd noises".

The folly, at the bottom of The Old Vicarage's garden

God! I will pack, and take a train,

And get me to England once again!

For England's the one land, I know,

Where men with Splendid Hearts may go;

And Cambridgeshire, of all England,

The shire for Men who Understand;

And of *that* district I prefer

The lovely hamlet Grantchester.

Brooke's phrase "Men with Splendid Hearts" has entered the English language and been used countless times since.

Grantchester is of course not a hamlet, as that word refers to a group of houses without a church, but Brooke presumably used the word as it sounded more evocative.

TO THE
GLORY OF GOD
IN LOVING
AND GRATEFUL
MEMORY
1914 - 1918

Grantchester's War Memorial in the churchyard. Brooke's name is listed among the dead, on one of the side-panels.
The roll of all the names is still read out every year in the Church on Remembrance Sunday, when those fallen in war are commemorated.

For Cambridge people rarely smile,

Being urban, squat, and packed with guile;

And Royston men in the far South

Are black and fierce and strange of mouth;

At Over they fling oaths at one,

And worse than oaths at Trumpington,

And Ditton girls are mean and dirty,

And there's none in Harston under thirty,

In the next 20 lines, Brooke names 13 nearby towns and villages and is mockingly rude about all of them. This light-hearted section contains playful humour rather than malice, and the place-names seem to have been chosen largely for their rhyming, as several were changed in the drafting of the poem.

As a member of the University Fabian Society, Brooke frequently bicycled around neighbouring villages delivering political pamphlets. This may be why he could recall so many of their names.

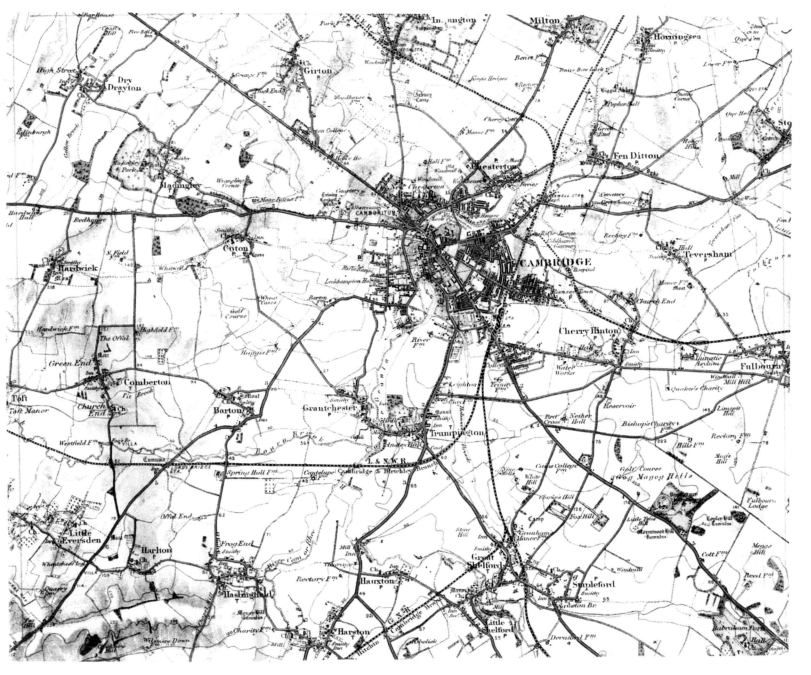

A contemporary Ordnance Survey map of Cambridgeshire, showing some of the surrounding villages mentioned by Rupert.
The general lack of settlements emphasises the rural character of the area at the time.

And folks in Shelford and those parts

Have twisted lips and twisted hearts,

And Barton men make Cockney rhymes,

And Coton's full of nameless crimes,

And things are done you'd not believe

At Madingley on Christmas Eve.

Barton, Coton and Madingley are to the west of Grantchester. Together with Grantchester, they now comprise "Barton Ward", an electoral ward of South Cambridgeshire District Council.

There is a story that, in the late 19th Century, the Squire of Madingley forbad his tenants from attending High Mass in church on Christmas Eve and, when they went anyway, he turned them out of their houses on Christmas Day.

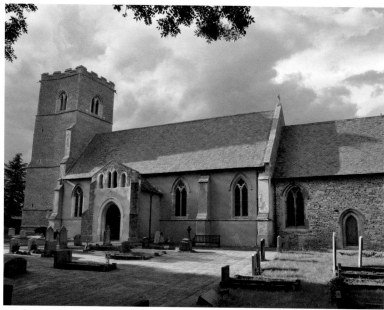

The ancient parish churches of Great Shelford, Barton, Coton and Madingley

Strong men have run for miles and miles,

When one from Cherry Hinton smiles;

Strong men have blanched, and shot their wives,

Rather than send them to St. Ives;

Strong men have cried like babes, bydam,

To hear what happened at Babraham.

There seems to be no historical basis for these final three claims. They close this humorous section of the poem, where Brooke roams over surrounding villages and lovingly mocks the inhabitants.

"The balk", a farm track leading from Grantchester towards Cambridge

But Grantchester! ah, Grantchester!

There's peace and holy quiet there,

Great clouds along pacific skies,

And men and women with straight eyes,

Lithe children lovelier than a dream,

A bosky wood, a slumbrous stream,

And little kindly winds that creep

Round twilight corners, half asleep.

Over the previous three pages, Brooke has aimed his mocking comments at the people who lived in the 13 villages that he names, rather than the places themselves.

He now turns his attention to the people of Grantchester. Ironically, it is unlikely that he had met many of them, as he did not mix much with the village, and confined himself to his lodgings, the river and his own group of fellow students and other friends. But he's trying to depict the ideal Grantchester of his nostalgia, and does so first by praising its inhabitants.

A "bosky wood" at the edge of the "slumbrous stream" of the River Granta

In Grantchester their skins are white;

They bathe by day, they bathe by night;

The women there do all they ought;

The men observe the Rules of Thought.

They love the Good; they worship Truth;

They laugh uproariously in youth;

(And when they get to feeling old,

They up and shoot themselves, I'm told) . . .

More praise for Grantchester residents, again given in a humorously-loving tone.

Grantchester Church, where villagers have been "worshipping truth" and God for nearly a thousand years since Norman times. It is unlikely that Brooke spent any time inside the church, for he was an agnostic, and once wrote in an outburst "I hate the Church of England".

Ah God! to see the branches stir

Across the moon at Grantchester!

To smell the thrilling-sweet and rotten

Unforgettable, unforgotten

River-smell, and hear the breeze

Sobbing in the little trees.

We're now into the final section of the poem. The previous section was light-hearted and amusing; Brooke now becomes deadly serious.

He lists longingly and from the bottom of his heart the many reasons he loves Grantchester. He starts with the trees and river.

A swan and her five cygnets swim on the river, having just left their nest by the mill-pond

Say, do the elm-clumps greatly stand

Still guardians of that holy land?

The chestnuts shade, in reverend dream,

The yet unacademic stream?

Brooke now moves on to a series of 12 questions, asking rhetorically whether the things he remembers are still there. The answer to all 12 questions was of course "yes", and in most cases remains so today (the chestnuts are still there, although the elms are not).

The stream is "unacademic" because Grantchester is upstream of Cambridge, and its waters have therefore not yet passed through the university town.

A photograph from the 1960s shows the clump of elm trees at the northern entrance to the village, which were killed by Dutch Elm disease in the 1970s

Is dawn a secret shy and cold

Anadyomene, silver-gold?

And sunset still a golden sea

From Haslingfield to Madingley?

And after, ere the night is born,

Do hares come out about the corn?

Anadyomene (pronounced ana-dee-om-eeny) is Greek for emerging or rising. The ancient goddess of love and beauty, Aphrodite (Greek) or Venus (Roman) was sometimes described as "Venus Anadyomene" or "Venus rising from the sea", because she was born by emerging from the sea – as most famously painted by Botticelli in The Birth of Venus *(1485).*

Brooke goes through the day, asking in turn about dawn, emerging from the night; about the sunset; and about night-time.

Normally shy animals, hares change their behaviour in spring, when they can be seen in broad daylight chasing one another around meadows

Oh, is the water sweet and cool,

Gentle and brown, above the pool?

And laughs the immortal river still

Under the mill, under the mill?

There are two pools on the river in the village – Byron's Pool and the Mill Pool – and Brooke seems to be referring to both of them in turn. He was a regular swimmer in both and, during the hot summer months, frequently refreshed himself in their "sweet and cool" waters.

Grantchester mill was large and very old, and straddled the river a hundred yards upstream from The Old Vicarage. It burnt down in 1928 and was rebuilt on a smaller scale as a private house.

A swan under the mill-pond bridge

Say, is there Beauty yet to find?

And Certainty? and Quiet kind?

Deep meadows yet, for to forget

The lies, and truths, and pain? . . . oh! yet

And now the final few questions, as the poem nears its end. Beauty, Certainty and Quiet would have been classical ideals greatly prized by Brooke; in contrast, lies, truth and pain would have upset him.

The harvest ripens in the fields around Grantchester in late summer

Stands the Church clock at ten to three?

And is there honey still for tea?

"Ten to three" was an invention, chosen to assist the rhyming. In fact, the church clock was broken, and the hands were stuck at 7.45 until it was mended in the 1920s.

And the honey? Brooke's landlord at The Old Vicarage was Mr. Neeve, who kept bees in the garden and sold it in the comb; it was particularly popular among the visitors to the Orchard tea-gardens next door.

The Church clock at ten to three, visible through the branches of the cherry and ilex trees that grace the churchyard

The Orchard tea-rooms open almost every day of the year, faithfully serving honey for tea, and are also home to the Rupert Brooke Museum